BRIAN COOK

An illini Legend

Brian Cook
with
Mark Tupper

SPORTS PUBLISHING L.L.C.
www.SportsPublishingLLC.com

Directior of production: Susan M. Moyer
Project manager: Greg Hickman
Developmental editor: Doug Hoepker
Copy editor: Cynthia L. McNew
Dust jacket design: Joseph Brumleve
Cover Photography: Mark Jones, UI Sports Information

ISBN: 1-58261-731-7

Printed in the United States.

SPORTS PUBLISHING L.L.C.
www.SportsPublishingLLC.com

To my mother, Joyce, and my family—
the best "team" a guy could ever have
—Brian Cook

For Lynn: my best friend, my wife
—Mark Tupper

Acknowledgments

This book would not be possible without the help of many people, not the least of whom are Brian and Joyce Cook, who exemplify all that's good about the love and teamwork that can exist between a parent and a child.

Additional thanks go to Brian's coaches: Neil Alexander, Donnie Aeilts, Lon Kruger, Rob Judson, Robert McCullum, Mike Shepherd, Bill Self, Norm Roberts, Billy Gillispie, Wayne McClain, Tim Jankovich and Jeff Guin. Over the years, each of these coaches has provided many insights into a special young man.

The 2002-2003 teammates of Brian's senior season also helped by sharing their thoughts. Those teammates are Jerrance Howard, Luther Head, Sean Harrington, Blandon Ferguson, "Big" Nick Smith, Roger Powell Jr., Dee Brown, Deron Williams,

James Augustine, Kyle Wilson, Aaron Spears, Jack Ingram, Nick Huge and Clayton Thomas.

At the University of Illinois, Kent Brown and Mark Jones once again delivered like the reliable pros they are. Thanks also to athletic trainer Rod Cardinal and secretary Cindy Butkovich, known by insiders as the people who actually run the Illini basketball operation.

I'd also be remiss if I failed to thank my sportswriting buddies John Supinie of Copley News Service, Herb Gould of the *Chicago Sun-Times* and Jeremy Rutherford of the *St. Louis Post-Dispatch* for their encouragement. This book was written during a time when the Illini basketball program was going through the turmoil of a coaching change, and it was through their help that I did not short-circuit while trying to handle two challenges at once. You guys are the best.

—Mark Tupper

Contents

Foreword

I think coaches remember all of their kids. I know I do. I can go back to Oklahoma State, where I was an assistant coach from 1986 to 1993, and I remember all of those guys, all of the players we recruited. But there are players who leave a larger impact on you than others, and that's only natural.

When we got to the University of Illinois, we saw players like Frank Williams, Sergio McClain, Cory Bradford and Brian Cook. And we said, "Hi, we're from Tulsa." But no matter what we'd done at Tulsa, those guys still looked at us and thought, "Who are these guys? What's the big deal about Tulsa?" But Brian was a guy who said, "Hey, Coach, glad to see you. Now let's get to work."

I will always remember Brian for making big shots, for us running poor offensive sets and throwing the ball to him so he could bail us out with two points, for putting freshmen on his back and carrying the team to a 25-7 record during his senior season. But I'll also remember him for what he did in practice, for diving on every loose ball and giving up his body.

Brian, by his attitude, allowed us to be good. He set an example. He sacrificed, and at times he was unselfish to a fault. Brian Cook has the best attitude of anyone you could ever hope to coach.

Above all, I'd say this: I would hope my son would mature and grow up to be a Brian Cook-type person.

—Bill Self, University of Illinois basketball coach, 2000-2003

CHAPTER ONE

On Top of the World

His smile had never beamed more brightly. His joy had never felt so right. As he climbed to the top of the ladder, Brian Cook felt like he was standing on top of the basketball world, at last.

His University of Illinois team had just won the Big Ten Conference Men's Basketball Tournament, beating Ohio State 72-59 at the United Center in Chicago. That's the arena Michael Jordan called home during his six National Basketball Association championship seasons with the Chicago Bulls. But on this Sunday afternoon in March, 2003, it was Brian Cook's home as he wrote a page of history with Illinois.

Once the game ended, wrapping up Illinois's first-ever Big Ten Tournament title, Brian raced toward the edge of the crowd and threw his long arms around his excited mother. As always, Joyce Cook wore Brian's Illini uniform jersey, No. 34, and sat close to the action. And as always, she was there for him. Nearly every significant moment in his life had been shared with his mother, and he wanted to make sure this would be no exception.

Moments later, Brian slipped a T-shirt over his uniform and a cap that hailed Illinois as the Big Ten Tournament champs over his sweaty head. He stood with his coach, Bill Self, alongside CBS announcers Jim Nantz and Billy Packer. As teammates

Brian Cook stands on top of the basketball world as he cuts down the nets after leading Illinois past Ohio State in the championship game of the Big Ten Conference Tournament. (Mark Jones, UI Sports Information)

huddled close and leaned their happy faces into sight of the camera, Nantz and Packer congratulated Brian on leading Illinois to the title. Brian's heart was pounding, and his smile only grew wider.

Then Brian's name was announced as the tournament's Most Valuable Player. Teammates grabbed him and hugged him and slapped him on the back. He helped hoist the golden trophy as thousands of Illini fans cheered from the United Center seats.

Then, for the first time in a basketball life that had earned many honors, Brian was sent up the stepladder to help cut down the nets, a traditional ceremony given to a team that earns a championship.

"It was a great moment," he said. "That's the first time in my life I've ever cut down a net. We went to the state tournament in high school but didn't win the title. We won two Big Ten championships, but both of them happened on the road and they don't let you cut down the nets on the road. So this was special. It was great for me."

Standing on the ladder, a stellar college career nearing its end, Brian Cook felt like he had reached the mountaintop. This was his team. This was his moment. Given an instant to reflect from his perch atop that ladder, he could see ahead to a bright and prosperous future. And he could look back in satisfaction on the challenging and sometimes difficult road that brought him here.

Joyce Cook has much to celebrate at the United Center in Chicago as Illinois wins the Big Ten Tournament title and son Brian is named tourney MVP. (Mark Jones, UI Sports Information)

2

The First Basket

Before he was a towering basketball giant, Brian Cook was like most three-year-olds. He was a playful little boy the day he ventured outside the modest Mississippi home of his grandmother's sister. Although just three, the memory is still clear.

"My Grandma Cook had a lot of family down South and we were down there visiting," he said. "There was a basketball hoop maybe 30 or 40 yards

When he was 17 years old, Brian wore a bow tie with his tuxedo at a dinner honoring McDonald's All-American players. Was he warming up here, at age four? (Photo courtesy of the Cook family.)

from my grandma's sister's trailer. I had a basketball and was out there playing and I remember throwing the ball up there and it went in the basket. I went running into the trailer and told my grandma, 'I made a shot! I made a shot!' I was so excited."

Many more would follow, but that was basket No. 1 for an impressionable youngster who had suddenly discovered a new talent.

That's not all Brian was realizing at a very young age. He realized his mother was usually working and his father was often away from home. Norman Cook had been a basketball star in his own right. He was a record-setting player at Lincoln High School in Brian's Central Illinois hometown of Lincoln. He went on to score more than 1,000 points at the University of Kansas and was a member of the 1974 Kansas team that reached the Final Four of the NCAA Tournament. In fact, Norman Cook was so talented that he left college after his junior season, becoming the first Kansas player in 16 years to leave school early to enter the NBA draft. The last to do it before him was Wilt Chamberlain.

Norm Cook was selected by the Boston Celtics in the first round of the NBA draft. But his NBA career lasted barely more than one season, and to continue playing basketball he tried to hook on with overseas teams.

But Brian's father was having other problems that were difficult for a young son to understand. He was suffering from a mental illness. He was in trouble with the police, and during the times he was at home he fought with Brian's mother and often did not treat her with respect. It made life at home uncertain and sometimes frightening.

As he grew somewhat older, Brian realized his father had a serious problem, and it would become an issue he, his mother and two sisters would deal with the rest of their lives. It was the kind of thing

Brian gets a lift from his mother in an off-road buggy. (Photo courtesy of the Cook family.)

people in Lincoln would whisper about, often in a cruel way.

"I remember pretty early some of the things people would say," Brian said. "Lincoln is a basketball-crazy town, and people knew my father didn't live up to their expectations. Because of that, a lot of people thought I would fail too. They expected me to fail."

That alone could make a young boy feel uneasy and afraid. But it didn't end there. Others teased him because his father was African American and his mother was Caucasian. "I remember one day I was with my mom at the Laundromat when a woman looked at me, then looked at my mother and made fun of us," Brian said.

"Some of that stuff was pretty bad," Joyce Cook said. "I had a lot of the racial stuff to deal with anyway. Norman didn't make it big like people thought he should have, and it was a bad go-around because people pointed a lot of it at Brian.

"But that motivated him. He didn't like people saying he was going to fail. He has never liked someone saying he couldn't do something. And that was one of the big things with me. I told him, 'We're going to show this town. We're going to show them who you are. You're going to make a name for yourself.'"

Brian during his grade school days in Lincoln.
(Photo courtesy of the Cook family.)

Keeping a Low Profile

He weighed just six pounds, nine ounces at birth, hardly a size that would predict a six-foot-10 adult. But by the time he was in the fifth grade, Brian began to notice he was taller than the other kids.

"It seems like I was always bigger than everybody else," Brian said. "I was taller and lankier and people would look at me and talk about me. I was different than everybody else. And people thought

Even as a youngster on the playgrounds and grade school gyms in Lincoln, Brian had All-Star potential. Here he models Michael Jordan's No. 23. (Photo courtesy of the Cook family.)

I was slow mentally. There was nothing wrong with me, but I was really quiet. I've always been kind of quiet around people."

In an effort to hide his height, Brian would walk at an angle, with his posture pitched forward. "I knew people were talking about my height and I wanted to make myself look shorter," he said.

"It must have been in the fourth or fifth grade, I remember walking into the Kroger store and my mom said, 'Boy, stand up straight.' So I started doing it and it felt totally different." It was his first lesson in body language, but certainly not his last.

It would be years before Brian would feel comfortable standing out in a crowd. But he began to change his posture about the same time he realized people were looking at him not just as a young person, but as a young basketball player. The expectations people had for him as an athlete, he understood, were beginning.

Although he had played recreation-league basketball as a very young boy, it was not until he was a fifth grader at Washington-Monroe Grade School in Lincoln that Brian joined his first school team. "I used to play outside all the time, and the guys I grew up with were telling me I should join the team," Brian said. "They had a little team that used to go out and play in tournaments all over and at the Lincoln Developmental Center. That's where I used to play and I loved it. I've loved basketball from then on."

In the fifth grade, Brian said most of his basketball-playing classmates were about five foot four or five foot five. He already stood six foot one.

At home, Brian was further realizing the frequent absence of his father. As a result, his mother was working many jobs, scrambling the best she could to keep food on the table and clothes on Brian and his two sisters, Kristina and Natasha.

"We were on public aid and I was working at McDonald's and as a nurse's aid at the Lincoln Christian Nursing Home," Joyce Cook said. "I was also taking some courses at Heartland Community College. So I was working, going to school and raising kids."

Thankfully, there were helping hands willing to pitch in. "I was with my Grandma Cook a lot," Brian recalled. "And my mom's stepmom, Grandma Myers. And my other grandma from Decatur, Grandma Kelley. My dad was gone a lot and we often didn't have much food.

"We had to make our way on things like eggs and rice. I remember a few times my mother would get a free meal when she finished working at McDonald's. She would bring home a Big Mac and cut it into three pieces, splitting it between me and my sisters. That would be our meal. We survived

Basketball wasn't always Brian's only sport. As a youngster, he took a swing at baseball with the local YMCA league. (Photo courtesy of the Cook family.)

on things like crackers with peanut butter and syrup sandwiches."

On occasion, Brian and his sisters would get into trouble around the house. "We'd get into all kinds of stuff," Brian said. "We'd color on the walls and stuff peanut butter down the vents. But that's because mom was off at work and my dad—when he was in town—was supposed to be watching us but he was off doing his own thing. So we had more chances to get into trouble."

Brian's mother dealt with those issues in her own way. And while providing for the family entirely by herself, she kept everyone fed and clothed. That wasn't always easy for a fast-rising son whose feet were now outgrowing a pair of shoes every five or six months.

I'm a Basketball Player

It would have been impossible for the citizens of Lincoln not to look at young Brian Cook as an athlete. His father had been one of the greatest basketball players in the city's history, leading Lincoln High School to the quarterfinals of the 1973 Illinois High School Association Boys State Basketball Tournament. He played at the University of Kansas and professionally with the Boston Celtics and Denver Nuggets.

Brian's uncle, Joe Cook, had been a football and basketball star at Lincoln High School and had played basketball at Duke University. His aunt, Stacey Cook, had been a multi-sport sensation who in the 1978 Class AA Girls State Track Championships finished second in the 440-yard dash to future Olympic gold medal winner Jackie Joyner of East St. Louis Lincoln.

Another uncle, Steve Cook, "was probably one of the greatest athletes ever at Lincoln," Brian said. And Brian's mother was an athlete herself. She was a sophomore on the girls' basketball team in 1978 when Lincoln High School reached the state tournament.

"With Norman and I both having played basketball, it was a given that our kids were going to have a ball in their hands," she said.

By the time he reached seventh grade, Brian understood there were two groups interested in his

Brian learned early on how to strike a pose as a basketball big shot while playing for the Lincoln Junior High School Trojans. (Photo courtesy of the Cook family.)

future. There were the doubters, who said he'd turn out just like his dad, full of disappointment and without a college degree.

And there were the supporters, of which there were many in Lincoln. One of his most enthusiastic supporters was his seventh-grade basketball coach, Donnie Aeilts, who himself had been a basketball star at Lincoln High School.

"I had heard quite a bit about him around town," Aeilts remembers. "When I finally met him I thought, 'Wow, this is really a wonderful kid.' He was an exceptional basketball player at that age. He was doing things most seventh-grade kids weren't doing, even though he was a little awkward because he was growing so fast.

"He could play point guard and bring the ball down the floor. He could play center, grab a rebound and take it from end line to end line, dribbling it behind his back. Even then you knew he was going to be something special."

Aeilts also knew that with Brian's family life, he needed some extra attention. With Brian's mother constantly working to support the children, Aeilts took it upon himself to help.

"I used to pick him up at his house and take him to Lincoln Junior High School every day," Aeilts said.

"Donnie Aeilts really helped me," Brian said. "He was more of a mentor than a coach. He always told me to do things the right way, to take care of my business. I could go over to their house and hang out with him and his wife, Michelle. As a matter of fact, when I was in high school, Michelle is the one who helped me study for my ACT test. I'd go over there every day after school and hang out and do homework.

"They'd make sure I got my homework done because my mom was working. Without them I might have just gone home and watched TV. But they were there for me all the time."

Don Williams, Brian's basketball coach in eighth grade, and Bob Verderber were others who became role models for Brian. And when his mentors weren't there, Brian could count on Grandma Myra, who still lives across the street from the Cook home. "She was always helping out with stuff like food or maybe a little money if I wanted to do something with my friends," Brian said. "It was like a group effort. But it was my mother who raised and disciplined me. And she was tough."

Joyce Cook may have been busy working and taking classes, but she found time to make sure her children understood there were rules to be obeyed. One of them was that schoolwork came before play time.

"She wouldn't let me get away with anything at all," Brian said, laughing about it now. "She'd always say, 'You think I don't know what you're doing, but I have people watching you.' Plus she's only 18 years older than I am. She'd been through a lot of the same things I was going through. You couldn't get much past her."

Brian found that out the hard way in junior high school when one of his grades slipped.

"The school called me and told me Brian had a D in a course," Joyce Cook said. "His team was playing in a tournament and I made him sit out. I told Brian he couldn't play with any Ds, so I told the coach he couldn't play until his grades went up. Then I went to the game just to make sure he didn't play."

Brian did not play. And although he was angry about it at the time, he said his mother's discipline made its point. "I was so mad at her. But I loved to play basketball and I realized I couldn't play if I didn't have good grades. So from then on, I made sure my grades were OK. It was either that, or sit. And I never wanted to sit."

Welcome to High School

Neil Alexander arrived in Lincoln in 1990 before Brian had reached his 10th birthday. Alexander was taking over as boys head basketball coach at Lincoln High School, charged with keeping alive a rich and winning tradition. Brian was only in grade school, but it wouldn't be long before Alexander began hearing about a growing young boy loaded with talent.

Brian loved his days with the Lincoln High School Railers.
(Photo courtesy of the Cook family.)

"I'm sure the first time I saw him was at one of our summer camps," Alexander said. "We took him to summer camp with us when he was in fifth or sixth grade and you could see the potential in him. The way he shot the ball and handled himself, you knew he had a lot of talent."

Brian said Coach Alexander wasted no time trying to develop his talents.

"As soon as I met him he started getting on me," Brian said. "He said, 'Get in the gym. Get in the gym.' He had me doing ball-handling drills and passing drills to get my hands softer. He had me shooting all the time."

Despite all the practice and potential, Brian's high school career started slowly. Although he was on the varsity roster as a freshman, he did not start. And during a practice before the start of his second season, a player rolled onto Brian's ankle, breaking it. The six-foot-seven sophomore fell to the court in pain.

Surgery followed, and for the first time since he could remember, Brian faced an extended time without playing basketball.

"We didn't know for sure if he'd be able to play basketball again," his mother said.

But by Christmas, Brian had recovered and was back on the floor, filling in where Coach Alexander needed him on the varsity team.

It was Brian's junior season when his basketball career clicked into high gear. Colleges already were aware of his potential, and on a very good, deep team, he was beginning to get the attention of recruiters.

"We won the King Cotton Classic in Arkansas and Brian was named Most Valuable Player," Alexander said. "After that things kind of took off.

He was about six-eight that season and he was still growing into his body. But that's when he started to believe in himself."

At the same time, Brian continued to hear comments from the doubters. His mother heard them too.

"You'd hear it when you were sitting in the stands," she said. "People would be talking and you'd hear them say, 'He ain't nothing. He's never going to do anything.'"

Those were words that stung a young teenager trying to do things the right way. They were bitter words that echoed in his head. But rather than react negatively to them. he let the insults be his motivation. "I kept telling myself, 'I'll show them. I'll prove all of them wrong.'"

And so he did.

He ended the college recruiting battle early by committing to the University of Illinois when he was still a high school junior. That made him a marked man as a senior, a special season in which Brian helped lead Lincoln back to the state tournament.

"After I committed, I had guys coming at me every night," he said. "They wanted to go after the guy who would be going to Illinois. I had double-teams and triple-teams every game. But I was fortunate enough to have a great shooter in Gregg Alexander [Coach Alexander's son] and other great teammates to take some of the pressure off me."

Brian averaged 21.7 points per game in a senior season that led all the way to the state tournament in Peoria. Hopes for a state championship were ended in a quarterfinal game when Warren eliminated Lincoln 59-43. "Still," Brian said, "it was great to get to the state tournament."

Brian didn't fully realize the impact of his final high school season until the senior awards assembly.

"I was just sitting there thinking I wouldn't be getting any senior awards. We had three-sport athletes and people like that who were going to get the awards. Then all of a sudden our principal announced over the intercom that Brian Cook had just won Mr. Basketball for the state of Illinois. The whole school stood up and gave me a standing ovation. It was great, man, just great."

Mr. Basketball is the most esteemed honor a high school player can receive in Illinois. It means he is considered the best high school player in the state. And over on the University of Illinois campus in Champaign, the Illini coaches were cheering just as loudly. They knew they were about to welcome a great addition to their team.

CHAPTER SIX

Choosing the Right School

Selecting the right college to attend can be an agonizing decision for a talented high school athlete. Brian Cook had many options. College coaches and recruiters closely followed his progress, and schools from coast to coast expressed interest. They offered scholarships, immediate playing time and the opportunity to face the best competition on national television.

"I got letters from just about everybody," Brian said. "Duke, Syracuse, Kentucky, Kansas, all the big ones. And all the Big Ten schools."

Those located far away were easily erased from his list. "I knew I wanted to be close to home," he said. "I took an unofficial visit to St. Louis University and my uncle took me to Arkansas. I also went to Marquette because I had family in Milwaukee and my cousin was going to Marquette."

But it became apparent early that Brian had an affection for one school in particular.

"He took only one official visit and that was to Illinois," said Lincoln High School coach Neil Alexander. "You could tell Brian felt that was the place to be. Brian was probably a pretty easy recruit because we sure didn't shop him around. [Coach] Norm Stewart from Missouri was here to see him. Clem Haskins from Minnesota showed a lot of interest. And we got calls from Duke and all your big ones. But you could tell where he wanted to go."

The University of Illinois campus is only a one-hour drive from Lincoln, and the Illini coaching staff used that to their advantage. Assistant coach Rob Judson stayed in close contact with Brian and Joy   g with Coach Alexander.

          ng attention to Brian in about

          w the head coach at

          le was a great pros-

          it the biggest thing

          he was such a sweet

ki   nce about him.

          uld tell the sky was the limit basketball-w   He was long and had such good skills. And he could really shoot the ball.

"[Illini coach] Lon Kruger and I went to Lincoln and visited Brian the first day we were allowed to go out recruiting. He was a huge priority for us."

College scouts from around the country were impressed with Brian's size and strength, but there was only one school for Brian: Illinois. (Mark Jones, UI Sports Information)

Brian instantly took a liking to Coach Judson.

"Coach Judson was great and he helped me make my decision," Brian said. "He's very Christian-oriented, a really loving guy. I knew right then when I met him that he was going to take care of me and he would fulfill the promises to my mother. It was an easy decision for me."

Making the college decision even easier was the lure of playing with other All-State players from Illinois.

"I committed right after Jerrance Howard committed," Brian said. "I liked Jerrance and I wanted to go with him. And Sergio McClain, Marcus Griffin and Frank Williams were all going to Illinois. Those guys won four state championships. You want to play with those types of players. Plus I took pride in being an Illinois guy staying in Illinois."

Brian said his mother encouraged him to look around. "But there was no doubt in my mind. I listened to my heart and I knew Illinois was going to be the right decision for me."

CHAPTER SEVEN

A Glimpse of the Big Time

Only the very best high school basketball players in the country are picked for the most elite recognition. And that happened to Brian Cook when following his senior season he was selected to play in the McDonald's All-American High School Basketball Game. At the time, he did not know many of the other players selected. Before long, though, those players would become household names in the world of college basketball and, a few years later, in the NBA.

The game was played in Ames, Iowa, and Brian was picked to the West team. He wondered whether he'd be able to hold his own against a collection of talent that included Nick Collison, Jason Gardner, Mike Dunleavy, DerMarr Johnson, Jason Richardson and Jonathan Bender.

"I roomed with Nick Collison," Brian said of the soon-to-be Kansas Jayhawk. "As it turned out, I'd room with him many times when we went on play for USA Basketball teams in international competition in Brazil and Japan. We've become really good friends."

Brian said he was nervous going into the game, not knowing how he'd measure up against the best high school seniors in the country. But he did extremely well, finishing with 14 points, 10 rebounds and three blocked shots in just 21 minutes of play. His West team won the game 141-118, and Bender scored 31 points to break the all-time McDonald's All-American Game scoring record that had been held by a young player out of North Carolina named Michael Jordan.

"That was a great experience," Brian said. "It helped my confidence to know I could play with those guys."

CHAPTER EIGHT

Off to College

He was 17 years old, stood six foot 10 and weighed a slender 215 pounds. At a glance, he may have seemed like a big young man. But Brian Cook was still a boy at heart, and when it came time to leave home for the University of Illinois, his heart was breaking. The same was true for his mother, who now faced the emotional prospect of parting company with her only son for the first time in her life.

To understand their relationship, Brian said it is important to remember that they are best friends. So saying goodbye—even if it meant only an hour's drive from home—was no easy matter.

"Brian leaving home has changed my life tremendously," Joyce Cook said. "It was a big deal for me to go through it. Brian and I have gone through a lot of things with his father that my daughters haven't experienced. He has been there for me through some real tough times. To have him leave was scary, and it was that way for both of us.

"The first day he left we were downstairs in his room and we were just bawling. But I had to be the strong one and tell him it was time to go. I remember dropping him off at his dormitory at college. He had this slow shuffle to his walk and his shoulders were down. He didn't want to go. And I cried the whole way home.

Joyce Cook is one proud mom as she celebrates Senior Night with Brian on March 9, 2003, over four years after she dealt with the emotions of losing her son to college. (Heather Jones, UI Sports Information)

"But I knew bigger things were going to come and we started to adjust that first year. We were on the phone with each other all the time, but I knew it was time for Brian to start doing things on his own."

If the adjustment to college life and being away from home was difficult, it was made easier because Brian was sharing his dorm room with Jerrance Howard, the point guard from Peoria, who already was his friend. And veteran player Sergio McClain, another Peoria player, helped show Brian the ropes. "Sergio took me under his wing," Brian said. "That really helped me."

Lon Kruger was the head coach, and Brian quickly discovered he liked his coach's demeanor.

"I think Coach Kruger is a great coach," Brian said. "I had no problems with him. I used to watch from the bench and see how he thought things out.

You could tell he is a great Xs and Os guy. But the thing I liked about him is that he didn't yell. But he just kind of told you and was positive about it. He had other guys who yelled at me, but not him. He was always positive about everything."

Even though he was taking a physical pounding in practice, Brian had no problems with the summer conditioning, and before long the official start of practice was approaching. It was early October, 1999, and the team would gather for its annual "media day." It's a time for the writers and broadcasters to visit with the players, talk about the upcoming season and pose for photographs.

In the team locker room, for the first time, Brian slid on his official Illinois game jersey. He admired it in the mirror, looking closely at the white, orange and blue uniform with his number, 34. Then, just to make sure it was his, he spun so he could see his back in the mirror. Sure enough, his name—COOK—was stitched across his shoulders.

Things were looking good, but the season had yet to begin.

CHAPTER NINE

it All Begins

Brian Cook's college basketball career started rather slowly, which may have been a good thing for a young kid still lacking in confidence. He came off the bench and played a few minutes here and there. "I really didn't do that much until Marcus Griffin got hurt and I took over the starting role," he said.

That breakthrough event happened on January 22, 2000, when Griffin, the center from Peoria, injured his knee in an afternoon shootaround just hours before a home game against Penn State.

Brian assumed Coach Kruger would choose a veteran to step in and start for Griffin. Someone like Victor Chukwudebe or Damir Krupalija, he guessed. But Kruger had another plan, approaching Brian and telling him, "You're in the lineup tonight."

There was a buzz around the Assembly Hall that evening as word spread of Griffin's injury and Cook's first college start. If anyone thought the weight of the occasion might make Brian too nervous to perform, they were wrong. Brian made his first six shots, pounded down three slam dunks and scored 20 points in an 87-76 Illini victory. He played so well that Coach Kruger would start him in the

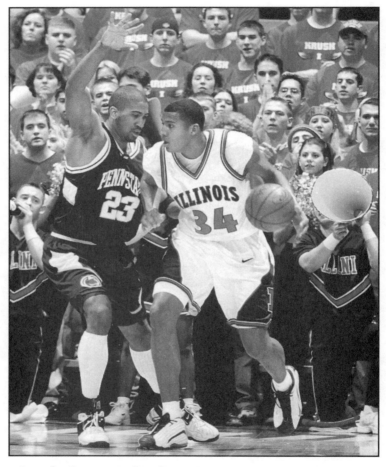

As a freshman, in his first career start on Jan. 22, 2000, Brian scored 20 points against Penn State. (Mark Jones, UI Sports Information)

final 17 games of the season. Brian shone, sharing Big Ten Conference Freshman of the Year honors with Michigan's LaVell Blanchard.

He was also named to the Big Ten All-Tournament team. But just when Brian appeared ready to give Illinois a big lift in the NCAA Tournament, his season crashed to a close with a painful ending.

The NCAA Tournament was an eye-opening experience for the young freshman. He looked awed and out of place. Brian was scoreless in a victory over Pennsylvania, then had just two points in a season-ending loss to Florida.

In the locker room after the defeat, Brian sat on a chair and hung his head. He had tears in his eyes, realizing he had not been prepared for the excitement of the tournament.

"The NCAA Tournament is different than the regular season," he said. "It's higher intensity with more media and more lights. You watch it on TV and you know that's where you want to play, but you don't know what you're getting yourself into until you've been there.

"These days freshmen are better prepared. They play in big summer tournaments all over the country. I'd never done that. When I got to the NCAA Tournament I kind of hit a wall. That Florida game was the most physical game I'd ever been in. Their center, Udonis Haslem, knocked the heck out of me and put me under the basket every time.

"I still go back and watch that tape and just say, 'Wow.' I use that tape as a motivation, remembering what it was like to be physically overmatched."

It would give him plenty to think about over the summer.

CHAPTER TEN

A Change at the Top

The news took Brian Cook by surprise. In late May, between Brian's freshman and sophomore season, Coach Lon Kruger assembled the team and said he was leaving the University of Illinois.

"He said he had a great opportunity in the NBA to become head coach of the Atlanta Hawks," Brian said. "He said he wouldn't have had that opportunity without us. He was pretty businesslike. He said what he had to say and that was it. We knew he was gone."

After hearing the shocking news, the Illini players met and talked about it. Ron Guenther, the university's athletic director, also met with the team, asking that they have confidence in his ability to find a new coach.

"He promised us he'd bring in a top guy and we knew he would," Brian said. "So we just worked and waited to find out who our new coach would be."

In early June, 2000, Cook and his teammates found out. Bill Self had coached the University of Tulsa to a 32-5 record the previous season, reaching the Elite Eight of the NCAA Tournament. The first meeting between Self and the Illini players took place in the team's meeting room at the Ubben Basketball Complex.

Brian racked up 25 points as a sophomore in the Illini's victory over Missouri in the annual Braggin' Rights game. (Mark Jones, UI Sports Information)

"He just came in and introduced himself," Brian said. "We knew he was going to get after us. That's the type of person he was. I liked him right away. And we found out Coach Judson would be staying. That really helped."

Shortly after he was hired, Self began looking at films of the Illini players, making some initial observations. He closely studied tape of Brian.

"I saw a guy with great talent who hadn't quite figured it out yet," Self said. "He was just like a newborn colt that once he gets up and runs he's going to be a champion. He just had to grow into his body and he would be as good as anyone."

Coach Self also saw the slumping shoulders, the hanging head and the same slow shuffle Joyce Cook had seen when she first dropped Brian off as a college freshman.

"My first year with him I probably spent more time talking to him about getting his shoulders back and his head up than anything else," Self said. "His body language gave the appearance that he was not confident. He seemed to defer to other guys all the time, which also indicates a lack of confidence."

Slowly, Brian's confidence began to build. In his sophomore season Brian raised his scoring average from 9.0 points to 11.2 per game. His rebounding average went from 4.5 to 6.1. And he started all 35 games as Illinois posted a 27-8 record, won the Big Ten Conference championship and was rewarded with the No. 1 seed in the Midwest Region of the NCAA Tournament.

There was great excitement surrounding that 2000-2001 Illinois team with Brian being joined in the starting lineup by Sergio McClain, Marcus Griffin, Cory Bradford and Frank Williams. The team also relied on a strong bench that included Robert Archibald, Lucas Johnson, Damir Krupalija and Sean Harrington.

Brian slams it down against Purdue during the Big Ten Tournament his sophomore season. The Illini won 83-66. (Jonathan Daniel/Getty Images)

Illinois beat Northwestern State and Charlotte in the first two games of the NCAA Tournament at Dayton, Ohio. That meant a trip to San Antonio, Texas for the Sweet 16.

Illinois's first opponent in San Antonio would be the University of Kansas and Brian's old roommate, Nick Collison. Behind Frank Williams's 30 points, Illinois won the game 80-64. Brian had just six points but was thrilled to be advancing to an Elite Eight showdown against the University of Arizona.

The Arizona game, however, was a nightmare. Williams struggled from start to finish. Brian played just 10 minutes, scored four points and fouled out. And one by one, his teammates fouled out as well.

"I remember half our team sitting on the bench having fouled out," he said. "I was mad, but I remember standing up the whole time, just cheering from the bench."

And even though Illinois made a late rally, Arizona won 87-81, ending Illinois's hopes of reaching the Final Four.

Becoming a Man

Through his first two seasons in college, the rap on Brian Cook was that he lacked the consistency and the physical strength to be a truly great player. He'd have a good half, then disappear. So better production and more consistency were the goals as he moved into his junior season. But 21 games into it, neither Brian nor the Illinois team were playing up to their potential.

At Seton Hall during his junior season, Brian erupted for 23 points and 15 rebounds to spark an Illini victory. (Mark Cowan, UI Sports Information)

About that time, a couple factors seemed to change everything.

Brian and his mother had agreed to be interviewed for a story to be published in *Sports Illustrated* magazine. The story would focus on how they relied on each other while dealing with a troubled home life caused by the erratic and often frightening behavior of Brian's father. It told of the trouble in great detail, and even Brian wondered how the public would react.

But after the story was published, Brian felt relieved.

"It helped let everyone know I hadn't been a kid who grew up with a silver spoon in my mouth," he said. "Everyone talked about how I was soft, but I've had my hardships too. I'd been through some real struggles. A lot of people didn't know about that. It lifted a lot of weight off my shoulders and cleared up some ignorance too."

Joyce Cook was grateful to finally have that story out in the open.

"It was important to tell them this is an illness Norman had. Maybe it would help someone who might be going through what I went through or help a kid who sees his parents going through it. It might let them know there can be a bright ending."

Coach Self said the story had an immediate impact.

"I felt after the story came out Brian thought, 'I don't have to worry about what other people are saying about my father's past. Everybody knows.' It was like a burden had been lifted off of him." At the same time the story came out, Brian and Coach Self had been meeting regularly, sharing informal talks and were quietly drawing Brian out of his shell. "He told me to stand tall, that I was an All-American," Brian said. "Coach Self put that in my head."

Brian Cook vs. Indiana's Jeff Newton: Two of the Big Ten's best inside players go head to head. Cook finished the Illini victory during his junior season with 15 points. (Mark Jones, UI Sports Information)

After the publication of the article in *Sports Illustrated*, Brian received a phone call from his uncle, Eric Jackson. "He said, 'Just go out and play like you did in high school. You don't have to worry about anything. Just go play.'"

So that's just what Brian did. Beginning on February 3 at Michigan State, Brian scored in double figures for the season's final 17 games. He became a powerful rebounder. Gone was the body language of an uncertain boy. Now he showed the confidence of a proud, self-assured man. With a victory at Minnesota on March 4, Illinois clinched its second straight Big Ten crown.

And even though Illinois would lose to Kansas in the Sweet 16 game of the NCAA Tournament, Brian Cook had sent a message: He'd be a force the whole country would have to deal with as a senior.

Sure, he may have been good enough to leave school early, as do many players who can't wait to get to the NBA. But Brian never gave that much thought.

"I loved college," he said. "And I promised my mom I'd get my degree. My dad never got his degree and I knew that was real important to her. So there was never any doubt."

Brian had great affection for all his teammates and coaches. Here, he sits on the bench at the conclusion of a big Illinois victory over Minnesota in the Big Ten Tournament during his junior season.
(Jonathan Daniel/Getty Images)

Going out in Style

Coach Bill Self knew Brian had come into his own when the Illinois team was going through a rough stretch during Brian's junior year. To try to get the team back on track, Self brought in a sports psychologist who worked on the players' confidence.

"He went around the room and asked each player to say something positive about their game,"

Self said. "Someone would say, 'I'm making 80 percent of my free throws,' or, 'I'm the best offensive rebounder.'

"Then he got to Brian and he said, 'I'm the best player on the floor every night.' And Frank Williams, who was surprised by that, said, 'No, you're not.' And Brian looked him right in the eye and said, 'Oh, yes I am.'

"Even though it was minor, I thought it was good he had the confidence to say something like that."

With Frank Williams, Robert Archibald, Lucas Johnson, Damir Krupalija and Cory Bradford gone, the leadership clearly fell on the shoulders of senior Brian Cook for the 2002-2003 Illini team. Long before the season began, he started showing that leadership. He became more vocal in the summer drills and worked hard with the five new freshmen.

Brian scored 22 points against North Carolina in the
first big victory of his senior season. The Illini rolled
over the Tar Heels 92-65 at the Assembly Hall.
(Mark Jones, UI Sports Information)

In October, at the Big Ten Conference Media Day in Chicago, each coach brought along two players for interviews. Cook strolled into the large meeting room wearing a shirt, tie and his Illinois letterman's jacket. As he walked in someone told him he'd been named Big Ten preseason Player of the Year.

"I hadn't even thought about it," Cook said of the honor. "But since a lot of players had graduated, I felt in my heart I was the best player coming back. So I guess I wasn't that surprised and the award motivated me."

Freshmen Dee Brown, Deron Williams and James Augustine joined Brian in the starting lineup. That's a lot of inexperience. Yet almost instantly there was something special about this team. Brown was a flashy guard, always talking and gesturing. Williams was steady and crafty with steals and assists. Augustine reminded many of a young Brian Cook—full of potential, lacking only strength and confidence.

Brian's senior season was a study in superb play and consistency, exactly what should define a senior All-American. His season scoring average of 20.0 led all Big Ten players and was the most by an Illini since Kendall Gill averaged 20.4 points in 1990.

Several games set him apart. Against Wisconsin on January 11 in the Assembly Hall, Brian made 12 of 19 shots and scored a career high of 31 points. In another home game on January 29 against Michigan, he almost single-handedly rallied Illinois from an 11-point second-half deficit to a 67-60 victory, erupting for 26 of his 30 points in a sparkling second-half performance. Desperately needing a victory on the road, Brian scored 26 points to help Illinois fight past Michigan 82-79.

Brian's career scoring high of 31 points came on Jan.11, 2003, against Wisconsin. (Mark Jones, UI Sports Information)

The biggest game, however, was played at Wisconsin on March 4, 2003. Win here, and Illinois would only need a victory at home against Minnesota to wrap up a third straight Big Ten championship. Lose, and the title would go to Wisconsin.

It was a hard-fought game played before a packed house at the Kohl Center. Wisconsin seemed to have the game under control, leading 59-52 with less than two minutes to play. But Brian drilled a three-pointer and freshman Dee Brown scored off a steal to make it 59-57 with less than a minute to play.

When Illinois got the ball back, Brian knew what to do.

"I got the ball and said to myself, 'I've been in this situation before.' I was thinking about the shot I missed against Kansas my junior year and I wasn't going to miss it this time. So I went to a turnaround jump shot. I wanted to take the shot. I wanted the responsibility. I wanted to win the game."

Brian's jumper with nine seconds to go swished through the net, tying the score 59-59. But with less than one second to go, Wisconsin's Devin Harris was fouled and made the second of two free throws, winning the game and the Big Ten title, 60-59, for the Badgers.

After some encouraging words from his mother, Brian said Illinois would use this loss as motivation to play well in the Big Ten Tournament. Eleven days and four victories later, Brian Cook stood atop the ladder at the United Center cutting down the nets that signaled Illinois's first Big Ten Tournament title.

The NCAA Tournament that followed was a disappointment. Illinois was sent to Indianapolis, where it had to play extremely hard to get past Western Kentucky in the first round. Brian had 17 points and 10 rebounds.

Jerrance Howard hugs the Braggin' Rights trophy as Brian and Sean Harrington rejoice after Illinois crushed Missouri 85-70 during Brian's senior year. (AP/WWP)

But in the second round, Illinois was upset by a red-hot Notre Dame squad that rained in a barrage of three-pointers. Brian played as hard as he ever has, grabbing 16 rebounds, more than in any game of his life. But he made just six of 23 shots and finished with 19 points.

"After the game I walked straight to the locker room," he said. "It was quiet. We were all hurting, hurting bad. Especially us seniors. We didn't want to go out like that.

"I shook everybody's hand. I went around the room and told each player I appreciated everything they had meant to me. I told them I loved playing with them. I told them it was a joy to come back my senior year and play with people I love. I gave every one of them a hug and told them they could learn from this experience. After I went around the room and thanked everyone, we were all bawling. Everybody."

It's not always easy to face the media after a difficult and emotional loss. But for nearly an hour Brian sat patiently at his locker answering every question. He made no excuses. He commended the play of Notre Dame. He wished he had shot the ball better. And then, with the faintest moisture in his eyes, he realized his college career had ended.

Of course the accolades had not ended. Brian would be named Player of the Year in the Big Ten Conference and was third-team All-American. He was one of 20 finalists for the James Naismith Award and one of 22 finalists for the John Wooden Award, both of which recognize the nation's top college player.

And at the 81st annual Kiwanis Men's Basketball Banquet, Brian would receive the Ralf Woods Award for free throw shooting, the Illini Rebounders Award, and the team's MVP award.

Four years ago he had arrived on campus as a slender, nervous, often homesick 17-year-old whose game wasn't quite ready for the big time. Now he was a strong, tall, confident 22-year-old, ready to greet the NBA.

Brian needed all of his 22 points against Minnesota on March 9, 2003—including this vicious dunk—to claim the Big Ten scoring title over Purdue's Willie Deane. (AP/WWP)

CHAPTER THIRTEEN

A Future So Bright

Every year since arriving on the University of Illinois campus, Brian Cook has been filling out a personal questionnaire given to him by the school's sports information office. It asks many questions, and some of the answers are used in its annual media guide.

He's consistently answered one question the same each time.

"Who's the most influential person in your athletic career?" His answer is printed in the media guide and says, "My mother, because she has done so much for me all through the years and I want to be able to give her back something someday."

Two days after losing to Notre Dame in the NCAA Tournament, Brian was enjoying one of his favorite hobbies—fishing. Then he and his mom began interviewing sports agents who would help manage his professional basketball career. The NBA draft was approaching in June, and somewhere in that first round, Brian Cook's name would be called.

Athletic trainer Rod Cardinal, who has cared for every ache and pain Brian has endured while at Illinois, smiles when he thinks about Brian's career.

"I'll remember him as the quiet, shy, bashful, not-much-confidence kid walking in the door," Cardinal said. "But I was talking to someone from

In Brian's final college game, he fought off double-teams to score 19 points and grab a career-high 16 rebounds in a second-round NCAA Tournament loss to Notre Dame. (Mark Jones, UI Sports Information)

the Orlando Magic about Brian the other day, and I told them how he has matured and how his leadership responsibilities have increased. He had good role models to learn from and he has become a good role model for our younger players. His growth from a kid to a man is what I will remember.

"I told the guy from the Magic that two things stand out for me. Brian is one of the few guys who would wear his Illini letterman's jacket on the road. He was proud of it. The other thing is that he's committed to walking across the stage on graduation in his cap and gown. He stayed in college four years and experienced everything he could. How proud his mom and grandma will be when he does that."

His high school coach, Neil Alexander, will be mighty pleased too. "I'm really proud of him and I think he's going to make Lincoln proud. Actually, they're already proud of him and they should be. He's a class act."

No one will be more proud of the next chapter in Brian's life than his mother and best friend, Joyce Cook.

"The thing I'm most proud of is the man he has become," she said. "You talk to him and the things he knows and the ideas he has. It's really something. The years he's been at Illinois, he has matured and grown up so much."

Brian looks forward to the day when he cashes his first NBA paycheck. He says he'll make good on his promise to take care of his mom. A house? A car? "Whatever she wants," he said without hesitation.

"No, that's his money," Joyce Cook said. "I've got my kids to take care of and they're not his responsibility, they're mine. He can make sure I can get to see him play, but he doesn't need to do any more than that."

When Brian was growing up in the shadow of a father who had fallen far short of very high expectations, Brian and Joyce Cook heard the doubters. They heard them say Brian would be no better, that he'd do no more.

"It's funny, when Brian is back in town there are a lot of people who give him thumbs up now," she said. "Everyone congratulates him. There are people I remember as plain as day who outright said this kid couldn't play ball. And now they're sending cards to our house congratulating him. It's kind of mind-boggling."

On the computer monitor in Brian Cook's apartment he has taped a precious keepsake, something that reminds him that dreams do come true. It's a cord from the net he cut down after winning the Big Ten Tournament.

"I see it every day," he said, still thinking about that climb up the ladder. "It makes me feel proud."

Other Great SuperStar Series
Titles from Sports Publishing!

The *SuperStar Series* includes books designed to appeal to younger readers. Athletes selected for this series are determined not only by their statistics and popularity, but also by their character. Sports Publishing takes special care to select only those athletes who are known to be community-minded and who possess the ability to be role models for the youth of this country.

Brian Cardinal: Citizen Pain
by Fred Kroner

Tim Duncan: Slam Duncan
by Kevin Kernan

Reggie Miller: From Downtown
by Joe Frisaro

Marshall Faulk: Rushing to Glory
by Rob Rains

Sammy Sosa: Slammin' Sammy
by George Castle

Dale Earnhardt Jr.: Born to Race
by Kathy Persinger

Jeff Gordon: Rewriting the Record Books
by Ken Garfield

Tony Stewart: Hottest Thing on Wheels
by Jim Utter

- **All books are 5.5 x 7 softcover**
  - **25+ photos throughout**
    - **96+ pages**
